The Four Immortal Chaplains:

Legacy of Virtue

By Cady Crosby

~Dedication~

This book is dedicated to the memory of Ben Epstein, Dorchester survivor. Mr. Epstein was committed to the Four Chaplains' story and became a part of their legacy himself.

Chapter 1

~The Wolf Strikes~

"It took quite a long time before [we] heard the detonation, and because of the hazy weather and heaving sea [we] didn't know what [we] were shooting and what [we] had actually hit."[i]

~Erich Passler, U-223 crewmember, speaking about the torpedo that hit the USAT Dorchester

The date is January 23, 1943.

You are an American soldier in World War II, preparing to leave on a mission to a secret destination. The ship that will take you on your journey is the USAT *Dorchester*. It will be a long, difficult, and dangerous trip.

You travel through Torpedo Junction, a section of the North Atlantic that is lined with German U-boats, known as wolf packs. Their job and greatest desire? To sink American transport ships.

On February 2, 1943, your journey is almost over. You are only hours away from your final destination: Greenland. Tensions are high and the anxiety is palpable.

Suddenly, the ship officer's voice comes over the intercom. An enemy German U-boat has been sighted and is following the *Dorchester*. All personnel are ordered to sleep fully clothed and in their lifejackets, boots, and parkas.

Uneasiness is now intensified. Some men stay up playing cards, trying to keep their minds off the danger. Others try to sleep despite the sweltering heat in the bowels of the ship. But the order to wear lifejackets and full uniforms is disregarded by most.

12:55 AM. February 3, 1943. The wolf strikes. The USAT *Dorchester* is torpedoed by German U-boat U-223.

The damage is crippling. Power is lost. The danger is extreme, and the abandon ship message cannot be sounded for lack of power. Chaos ensues. Men who survived the torpedo blast all rush up from below deck, scrambling up the stairs in the thick darkness. A blast of cold air hits them as they reach the top deck and each is confronted with a stunning realization- the majority are not wearing lifejackets, their only hope for survival.

Soldiers are now screaming, crying, threatening, looking for some hope of survival. Returning to the darkness below to secure a lifejacket is impossible because of the water below decks.
But suddenly, you see four men. These men are not screaming, crying, or threatening.
John Washington, a Catholic priest.
George Fox, a Methodist minister.
Alex Goode, a Jewish rabbi.
Clark Poling, a Dutch Reformed preacher.

The four chaplains have been with you during the entire voyage. During those long days and nights, they offered spiritual solace and a friendly ear. Each of the four did whatever he could to soothe everyone onboard and to encourage you in your dreams and hopes. Now, in the midst of impeding death, they assumed a different role- that of rescuers. You see them handing out lifejackets from a locker on deck. You watch as frightened men form a line leading to the locker and the chaplains.

You step into line.

The line moves quickly as the ship slides down into the water. Men scramble to get closer to the chaplains, to seize the lifejacket that is their only chance of safety. You watch as several men try to break the ice that holds the lifeboat pulleys frozen in their davits. One is cut away; it immediately falls off the side of the ship and sits, overturned, in the water. Another is hacked away, this time successfully, and a few men scramble into it.

By this time, you're near the front of the line. There are still at least a hundred men behind you, but it doesn't matter anymore. Just as the man in front of you secures a lifejacket and runs to find a seat in the lifeboat, Chaplain George Fox reaches into the locker and then turns to stare at you, horrified. You both realize the frightening truth--- the locker is empty.

Without a word, Chaplain Fox unties the laces of his jacket with frozen fingers. Then he pulls the lifejacket over your head, claps you on the shoulder, and says simply, "Godspeed." With that, you move forward, unable to believe what has just taken place. You turn around, only to see the other three chaplains handing their lifejackets to three other men like yourself. You each were just handed a chance at life in a split-second decision; and that decision would change your life forever.

***

The story of these four chaplains aboard the USAT *Dorchester* is not a fairy tale, nor is it an old legend. It is a story of real men, real disaster, real hope, and real courage.

To better understand the story of these four chaplains, it's important to see them first as individuals. Only then is it clear how heroic their sacrifice was, and how deep the bonds of their friendship.

Chapter 2

~Clark Poling~

"I knew he was thinking of the more difficult and as he regarded them, the more dangerous duties of armed conflict. He couldn't think of himself in a softer or more protected place than some other man or accepting a special consideration."[ii]

~Dr. Daniel Poling, Clark's father

"All right team, good game. Have a great night and we'll go over specifics on Monday."

Clark Poling, still panting and out of breath from the football game he had just played, stumbled back with his family to the car. His father, Daniel Poling, looked toward his son worriedly. "Feeling alright, Clark? You played well tonight."

Eleven year old Clark nodded. "I'm okay, just a little frustrated. I'm not nearly as big as any of the other fellows on my team and I'll never be able to play as well as them. I'm too small and slender." His stepmother put an arm around Clark and hugged him. "You're an excellent team-player, dear. Don't feel down about it."

Clark still questioned his worth on the team, but that wasn't unusual for him. Clark questioned almost everything- his religion and his self-worth to name a few. But his questions usually led him to a deeper understanding about whatever it was he wondered. And it was for this reason that Clark's father, a well-known minister, encouraged Clark in his questions.

Clark's older brother, Daniel Jr, was not so welcoming of his younger brother's struggles. One afternoon, Daniel finally erupted at Clark's constant line of questioning. "Clark, how do you even call yourself a Christian with that kind of attitude? Dad, make him stop asking questions like that about God!"

"What was he asking about, Daniel?" their father came over to stop the argument.

Clark spoke before his brother in order to defend himself. "All I said was that I was reading the Bible this morning and came across some things that I wonder about-"

"See, Dad? He's being a heretic, thinking that way!"

Their father put a firm but gentle hand on the older boy's shoulders and looked at him. "Daniel, you and your brother are very different. You are an accepter- you receive and believe what you've always been taught. Clark inquires, but that doesn't mean he doesn't believe. His questions sometimes lead him to a deeper belief."

Clark smiled at his father, glad that he was understood, while Daniel fumed. But even with their differences, the two brothers usually got along well, getting into all sorts of mischief together.

Clark's life, though usually happy, was not always easy. When he was about four years old, his father had gone to fight in World War I and didn't come home until the war was over. The Poling family had gotten along without him, but all were beyond joyous to have him home again.

But their rejoicing wouldn't last long. Clark's mother, Susan, contracted tuberculosis and died several days after Dr. Poling was home. The loss affected Clark deeply; he was only eight years old at the time. When a new mother came into the home, she embraced and loved the children as her own, and Clark was able to look to the future again.

As he grew older, school became a top priority for Clark, and he was able to find more answers to his questions. Since he went to a Quaker school, the teenager was able especially to discuss pacifism, a subject close to his own heart.

"I've been thinking about the ethics of war, Tommy," he said to one of his friends at school.

The other lad looked up from where he was reading. "Thinking about it again? You already had a long discussion about it in class today."

"I know, but I still think it's not as clear-cut as simply not fighting. I mean, sometimes war is a 'necessary evil'; something that we would want to prevent but must participate in to stop the root problem."

Tommy nodded but was still confused by his classmate's ideas. "But Clark, you realize that that isn't exactly pacifism."

"Yes, I know. I guess I'm not completely a pacifist, though I agree with most of their basic concepts. The concept of pacifism is good, but I believe that war is justifiable when defending yourself."

Clark continued while at school to study as much as he could. His father was pleased by his son's ability to think and ask questions and encouraged his search for truth.

As a young man, Clark decided that he wanted to be a minister. He enrolled at Rutgers University, where he pursued his dream with vigor. But Clark also fostered a deep love for the poor and disabled in the school community. While there, he met a blind Jewish boy and they became fast friends.

"How are you able to prepare for tests?" Clark asked one day.
The younger boy shrugged amiably. "Sometimes I'm able to ask my roommate to read the textbook for me, but often he's not available. So the professor will review the concepts from class with me once in a while, and I try to take in the information again. But mostly, I try to be a really good listener."

"How about I read for you each day?" Clark suggested. "You'll be able to study much better and score higher, I'm sure."

The student raised his eyebrows in surprise at his friend's generosity. "Thank you, Clark, that's incredibly kind of you. You don't know how indebted I am to you."

On December 7, 1941, everything suddenly changed. Clark heard the radio announcement while studying at the church office after Sunday service. He came rushing home to his wife and little boy. He found his wife leaning across their kitchen counter, still listening intently to the radio. She looked up at him with fear, grief, and terror in her eyes.

Clark came to her and wrapped his arm around her shoulders. He didn't say a word, but Betty knew what he was thinking. "You must go, Clark. I know how you feel about it all, and I know that you don't want to leave us. But you cannot defy your conscience."

He breathed a deep sigh of relief, glad to not have to tell her. "Thank you for understanding, darling. I want to tell my father before I sign up."

They went over the next evening for dinner, giving Clark the opportunity to talk with his father, who himself was well-known pastor, about his decision. "Dad, I want to enlist, but not as a chaplain."

Dr. Poling joked in reply, "Oh, are you too afraid?"

Surprised at the joke, Clark raised his eyebrows. "Of course not! What makes you say that?"

"Chaplains are not armed- they don't carry weapons. They aid the soldiers by ministering to their bodies and souls, often on the front lines. They have one of the highest mortality rates. I thought perhaps you might be too scared to be in such a dangerous job."

Dr. Poling knew that the opposite was true. Clark wanted to be in the most difficult position which he had previously considered to be an armed soldier. With the information his father had given him, Clark decided he would become a chaplain and enlisted soon after their conversation. He finished training and was then sent to Camp Myles Standish to await further orders.

Chapter 3

~Rabbi Alexander Goode~

"Rabbi Goode's influence directly or indirectly touches every primary school and high school in the state. In this regard at least his life goes on in a wider sense among the young men and women of our nation, and it is only a question of time until his name is remembered everywhere."[iii]

~Victoria Lyles, superintendent of primary education in New York

"Alex, please come downstairs, I need your help with dinner."

The studious young boy looked up from where he was reading, leaned back in his chair, and called down, "Mother, I'm close to being finished with this book. May I please have five minutes to finish it up?" He heard his mother's heels clicking on the stairs and sighed, knowing what the answer would be.

"Alexander Goode, please go downstairs immediately." Fanny Goode stood in the doorway, hands on her hips, frowning at her eldest son. "I need to be at a gathering in about an hour and don't have any time to make dinner."

"Yes, Mother." Alex stood up and moved downstairs. He was a good cook and was happy to help his family, but was growing weary of being called away from his studies to take care of things around the house. His mother often distanced herself from her family of four children, and the responsibility fell to Alex to take care of his siblings. She and his father had divorced years before, and Fanny wasn't able to relate well with her scholarly, athletic son.

Alex excelled in almost everything he did. He was built to play sports and got along well with his teammates. School came easy to him on most days, and even when it didn't, he tended to enjoy the work. That was something his mother simply could not fathom.

"I don't understand, Alex. You are constantly in your room, reading books, and now you tell me that when you graduate, you'll leave your family behind to study more?" Fanny crossed her arms at the dinner table. Alex had just told her about his college plans.

Alex leaned over to clean up the milk that his youngest brother had spilled. "Mother, you're twisting my words. I do want to study more, but it'll be a benefit to the family. I want to be a rabbi and that will be an honor to all of us. College is the first step in that process."

"How are you planning on finding the money to go to school? Is there money in this home that I don't know about?" her voice rose as she became more intense about the topic.

Alex put his hands up to soothe his mother and smiled at her gently. "It's all right Mother, there's still a couple of years until I graduate. That's plenty of time to make plans."

In spite of his mother's opposition, Alex didn't let go of his dream. He continued to be the star of his class, even creating his own formula for algebra in order to solve problems more quickly. School did not shield him from the real world, however. As a Jewish male in the wake of the First World War, Alex often had to combat anti-Semitism. He did not have as much of a problem as his siblings did, and often shielded them from the unkind remarks and cruel blows that came their ways.

One day, his younger brother came home upset. "I don't understand it, Alex! Why is it that just because of our faith, we are treated so differently?"

Alex put away his book to answer his brother's honest question. "I don't know, Moses. We shouldn't be treated differently; all men deserve dignity, no matter their color, race, or religion. Unfortunately, many groups of people are still struggling with injustice even here in our country."

This reminded Moses of his older brother's own struggles with injustice. He looked up at Alex and fought back tears as he asked, "Did the bullies who attacked you and Joseph last week say why they hated us so much?"

Alex cringed at the painful memory. Several youths had all ganged up on him and his brother the week before and the two boys had come out of the situation with numerous blows and cuts. Even more hurtful than the physical scars, however, were the derisive words with which the boys had been taunted. It hurt Alex to think that Moses, his youngest brother, had encountered the same foul treatment. "No, they didn't. There's no real reason for their treatment, Moses. They've simply been raised to be that way. It's our job to combat their brutality with kindness. Hitting back will never solve the problem."

The anti-Semitism that Alex and his family grew up with molded him into a young man always mindful of the world around him. It kindled a desire in him for all men to be at peace with one another. Alex believed strongly that education would help bring about that reality- and Alex loved learning.

Shortly before graduation, Alex found a new love in the person of Miss Theresa Flax. She was beautiful, talented, and perfect for Alex. One day, he found an opportune moment to speak to the shy girl. "Miss Leesen, I've forgotten my book," was Alex's excuse one day as he entered the classroom.

"It's all right, but do try not to make the mistake a habit. Please look on with another student."

Alex walked over to where Theresa was sitting, her brown hair shadowing her face. "Theresa, I forgot my French book this afternoon and Miss Leesen suggested that I look on with you."

"Oh…I'm sorry that you forgot the book," Theresa said quietly. She was shy and had difficulty making new friends. But she liked Alex well enough to share her book.

At a dance soon afterwards, Theresa observed that Alex, though proficient in most areas, was not naturally gifted at this social skill.

"Alex, would you like some dancing lessons?" she offered at class the following week. "I think that you could be good at it, with some practice. I can teach you."

Alex's face lit up at this prospect. It meant more time with the girl he loved and this initiative on her part both thrilled and emboldened him. "I'd love to take dance lessons from you, Theresa. But I would want to repay you in some way; would you like tennis lessons? I can teach you."

The lessons helped in advancing their relationship and after they both graduated high school together, Alex asked Theresa to marry him.

"Oh, Alex, we can't be married yet," said Theresa sorrowfully. "I've just found a job at the White House, as a secretary. It's a good-paying job, and I'd have to leave it if we were married."

"We could live off of my income," Alex protested.

She shook her head. "You don't *have* any income, Alex. You're going to rabbinical school and won't have much time for work. No, this is not the time to marry. Finish your studies first; follow your dream; then we'll talk."

So Alex, sad but aware of the fact that Theresa was probably right, left for Cincinnati, Ohio. While there, he continued to foster their relationship, writing pages upon pages of letters. Alex wrote a letter almost every day and told Theresa about all of the activities he was undertaking- debating, public speaking, and athletics. "My year would be complete if I won a couple of the essay prizes, the oratorical contest and the tennis tournament. Really small things but they inspire one to do bigger things."[iv] The amount of time and training Alex put into these activities was intense, and his successes were gratifying.

Finally, early in 1935, Theresa said "yes" to Alex's continued marriage proposals. He wrote to her ecstatically, "I may be delirious with joy now, Sweet, but I know how much I love you, surely more than [any] man loved maid before, and all I can say is a thousand times 'I love you'…I'm walking on air."[v]

After their marriage in July of 1935, Theresa and Alex were finally together. Alex was still looking for work and struggling to make ends meet. His plans were to finish school and then proceed on to finding a temple to accept him. After graduation, Alex and Theresa moved to New York, Alex applied at a temple nearby and was accepted. Calling the president of the temple afterward, he soon discovered a new privilege and responsibility of his chosen profession.

"Hello, Mr. President, how are you? This is Alex."

"Alex?" There was an uneasy pause on the other end. He continued several moments later. "Rabbi Goode, people in this town are funny. They want to be sure to respect their rabbi, and that their rabbi knows the importance of his position. You must get used to being known as Rabbi Goode, not Alex. From now on, that is your name."

Alex sat for a moment, surprised by the president's words. Then he thought to himself, "I've always wanted to be a rabbi. Now that I am a rabbi, I guess I had better get used to being called by my proper title." So he replied, "Then yes, this is Rabbi Goode."

Alex was thrilled to be able to fulfill his life-long ambition and support Theresa. Soon enough, they were also providing for their daughter, Rosalie. Life could not have been better. Alex and Theresa loved their congregation, their daughter, and each other, and everyone loved their new Rabbi Goode.

Alex started a Boy Scout troop, and his Scouts were the first that, from the same troop, earned various multi-cultural awards. He had some Jewish boys, some Catholics, and some Protestants. This was uncommon at the time but was consistent with Alex's desire for everyone to be treated equally. Many times his mind raced back to his conversation with young Moses: "There's no real reason for their treatment, Moses. They've simply been raised to be that way. It's our job to combat their brutality with kindness." *What better way to do that than through the Boy Scouts*, thought Alex.

But on the morning of December 7, 1941, when Pearl Harbor was attacked, Theresa's heart sank. She sensed that her loving husband, so intent on peace and goodwill, would feel that in this case, the best way to accomplish peace would be to serve other soldiers in the war. Theresa was right. When Alex came home that evening, he looked at his wife and daughter, and said gently, "Theresa, I want to enlist."

I know, Alex," she said tearfully. She'd prepared herself all afternoon for the statement, yet it was still difficult to hear. "Do what God wants you to do."

Alex enlisted as a chaplain the day after their conversation. He was soon transferred to Philadelphia, where he waited with others at Camp Myles Standish for orders. Although he missed his family, he wanted nothing more than to serve his country in the most direct way possible. Alex could hardly wait to be sent overseas.

Chapter 4

~George Fox~

"He was a happy-go-lucky fellow, and he just fit in with everything. If he could help you in any way, he would. He used to make ice cream for the family, and he could do anything- climb up roofs and paint and help out with housework...he really gave us a wonderful time."[vi]

~Oliver Fox, George's adopted brother

"George! Get in this house now!"

The gruff yell echoed across the yard. The teenager sighed dismally, knowing what he would face when he got in the house. Nevertheless, he put down the axe he was using to chop wood and walked toward the stairs.

At seventeen, George was used to his father's abusive treatment. But just because he was used to it didn't mean he was willing to put up with it forever. As he'd grown older, George vowed to himself that he would run away from home whenever it became possible.

When the United States entered World War I in April 1917, George immediately saw his chance. He regretted the fact that he would have to leave his loving mother and siblings behind but knew the time was right. Running to the enlistment office, George joined the U.S. Army.

On the ship heading toward France, he joined in his fellow soldiers' dreams about the future. "Where are you hoping to be stationed?" a stranger asked him while they were chatting onboard.

George shrugged his shoulders. "Somewhere full of action. I don't want to just sit and do nothing. That's not why I signed up."

But the action that George sought didn't come from shooting bullets at the enemy. Instead, he joined the ambulance corps and was given a more compassionate assignment- to help transport wounded soldiers from the battlefield to safety. It ended up being the perfect job for an emotionally deprived young man who had never received love from his own father. George earned multiple medals for his work. But that all ended when he himself was wounded one day. A field hospital collapsed and crushed him, turning the medic into a patient himself.

"Where am I? What happened?" George asked when he finally awoke in a French hospital.

"You have some severe spinal injuries," the doctor said and leaned over to check his heart rate. "You were hurt rather badly when the building you were in came crashing down upon you."

George tried to sit up, but fell back in frustration when he found that he physically could not. "How soon do you think I can get back to the field?"

"The war's over, son. It ended five days ago."
The news stunned the wounded George. Where would he go now?

He couldn't go back to the house in Lewiston, Pennsylvania that was not a home to him. Instead, he found another option in the family of Percy and Florence Fox. During the war, Florence, wanting to encourage the soldiers on the front lines, had picked a few young men's names out of the newspaper and sent them letters and care packages. George was one of those she picked, and he and Florence carried on a lively correspondence for many months. After his recovery, George packed his bags and went to the Fox's home in New York for a visit.

The weeklong visit turned permanent as George was adopted by the Fox family. It began a time of happiness and joy that he had never known before.

"George, will you tie up this swing for us?" one of his new sisters called. She was trying to reach a tree branch that was far too high for her small stature.

George came over and swung her around. "Of course I can! You should've called me earlier." After tying the small ropes, George told her, "I'm making ice cream just now, would you like to have some?"

His sister squealed in delight and abandoned the swing to help her big brother. Life was never so good for George.

But eventually, George decided that he wanted to do something more than simply stay at home and nurse his wounds. So, packing his bags, he headed off to the Moody Institute, where he met Isadore Hurlbut. George loved her on first sight and contrived a chance to speak with her at the earliest opportunity.

"Hello there," he said cheerfully. "I'm George. Do you have someone to walk you back to your dormitory?"

The attractive young woman looked up at him, surprised. "Oh! I'm Isadore, and no, I don't."

"I'll walk with you, if you like," said George, counting on the fact that it would have been rude for her to say no. So, they walked back together.

The two ended up walking together many times afterward, and Isadore found that she didn't mind it at all. Her favorite walk was when they walked downtown together to find an engagement ring for her.

But Isadore's sister was not as thrilled about her engagement. "Have you thought about the fact that you are engaged to a crippled man? You will probably have to take care of him. He doesn't even have a paying job."

Because of these stinging remarks, the engagement was delayed for several months. But in time, Isadore could no longer ignore her love for George and they were married soon afterwards. In turn, George again made a vow to himself- that he would unconditionally provide love and support for his wife.

But this vow meant that George had to leave school and accept a job as an accountant in order to fulfill his promise. Life progressed naturally and happily for a while, until George's conscience began to prick him.

"I know I'm called to be a minister," he told Isadore one evening after work. "My job as an accountant isn't what I'm supposed to be doing."

Isadore, understanding of the need for her husband to follow his conscience, smiled uncomfortably at him, showing her worry.

Finally, after their son Wyatt was born, George was appointed a pastor of a Methodist church. All was well for a short time, and a daughter, Mary, soon joined the Foxes. George felt he needed additional education to become a better minister. Isadore and George struggled together over the decision, but eventually decided that God was calling him back to Boston University, where he had previously finished his studies.

Several long, hard years followed. Studying took up most of George's weekdays, and on weekends, he preached at two local Methodist churches. Making ends meet wasn't just hard, it was almost impossible.

One day, a member of the church's board announced to the Foxes, "George, we're giving you a promotion. You are being sent to Union Village, a town in Vermont."

But the 'promotion', it turned out, was exactly the opposite. George's pay would actually be reduced in this new assignment. His wife, outraged at the unfair difference, asked George, "How can you be so nice to them?"

"Let's just not let them know that we know the difference," he told her gently, hoping his wife would continue her support for him as a pastor. Isadore was amazed by her husband's kind heart, even to those who hurt him, and tried to continue to help him in any way she could.

But when his daughter came home crying from school one day, even George became angry. "What happened?" he asked, turning to his son.

Wyatt was spitting mad. "Some bullies at school were mean to Mary. They tore her dress and said rude things."

George, just as mad as his son, decided to preach a sermon the following Sunday on the effects of anger and gossip. The subject didn't sit well with the board, who reprimanded him severely. This certainly was not where God wanted him, George concluded, and so the family moved to Gilman, Vermont. This move proved to be a stroke of Providence, and George's new congregation absolutely loved him.

On December 7, 1941, everything changed for George. The news was announced on the family radio and George leapt up. "Now we will get them!" He turned to his wife. "Of course Isadore, you know I must enlist."

"You are still wounded from the last war," she reminded him. "I don't know how you're planning to serve."

George shook his head emphatically. "No, I'm not planning on being a soldier. This time, I'm going in as a chaplain." He wanted to continue to bring the news of God to all he came in contact with, including those in battle.

So, after training, a new chapter of life began for George Fox. He was assigned to train at Camp Myles Standish and from there, eagerly awaited orders of where God would send him next.

Chapter 5

~Father John Washington~

"He was a happy person and thought all priests were naturally happy. He never asked me to become a priest. He sold me by example. I wanted to be happy, too."[vii]
~Edward Sullivan, one of Father Washington's students

"We interrupt our Sunday afternoon broadcast to bring you this special news bulletin. The Japanese have attacked Pearl Harbor, Hawaii by air, President Roosevelt has announced. The attack was also made on all Naval and Military activities on the principle island of Oahu. We take you now to Washington…" Static followed the grim message.

"What does it mean, John?" The elderly woman looked over at her son for support. The man, dressed in clerical robes and a Roman collar, slowly backed the car into the driveway before responding to his mother.

"It means that the Army will need all available men," Father John Washington told his mother. He came around the car and opened her door. "I'm sorry that I'm not able to stay for tea, but I must get back to the church. You know that I must enlist."

After walking his mother in, kissing her, and locking her door, John drove away. He didn't have to think twice about what his role must be; he knew he wanted to aid his country in the best way possible. As a Catholic priest, Father John Washington would enlist as an Army chaplain.

It was natural for the Irish priest to make a firm decision quickly. From a young age, John had been raised to respect all around him and to care for everyone in trouble. Growing up as the oldest of seven siblings, John was a happy-go-lucky little boy who occasionally got into some arguments with his family and his friends. Known as Johnny to his friends, he was the leader of his neighborhood group of boys and they all looked to him for encouragement in their games.

John excelled in school. When at seven he was preparing to receive his First Holy Communion, those around him noticed how earnestly John engaged in his lessons. The important day finally came, and John's young heart was overflowing with gratitude and joy. After the ceremony, John ran up to his parents and told them eagerly, "When I grow up, I want to be a priest!"

A year later, the future priest was every bit a lover of fun and adventure. He loved imaginative play and shared his enthusiasm with his friends. One warm summer night, eight year old John went 'big game hunting' in the alleys of Newark with a couple of his friends.

"Johnny! Over here!" A whisper came from across the street.

"If there's a lion over there, we'll need to be extra careful," John reminded his companion, and then began to move stealthily behind a trash can. He held his BB gun close, in case one of the 'African animals' suddenly leapt out at them. But before he had a chance to think, something else leapt out at John.

"Ow! Quick, go get my ma....I really hurt my eye!"

The BB gun had discharged right by John's face and the BB had grazed his right eye. John would never be able to see clearly out of it again. A pair of spectacles aided John in seeing the world around him after his unfortunate accident. The glasses, however, made playing with his buddies a bit more difficult. Jeers from the group about looking feminine grated on John, and he often tried to solve his problems with his fists, a habit that drew the attention of his Irish Catholic mother.

"Showing that you can fight won't prove anything, John," his mother told him after he came in bleeding one afternoon. "You have to make yourself a better person, and people will love you for that. You'll only make enemies this way."

John winced as the wet cloth made contact with his face. "I'm already doing well in school, and they still tease me."

"The fact that they're teasing you speaks more to who they are than who you are. You can't respond in kind; you can show these boys the love and mercy that God has shown you."

It was a difficult truth for a young boy to handle. But John had been catechized well and knew that if he truly did have a vocation to the priesthood, he had to begin treating as others as a priest would. So the next time that the boys treated him cruelly, John shrugged it off, and in doing so, won the respect of many boys.

As John Washington grew up, he became more and more certain that God was indeed calling him to the priesthood. After graduating from Seton Hall Preparatory School, he completed his undergraduate studies at Seton Hall University and in 1931 entered Immaculate Conception Seminary at Darlington, New Jersey.

"What are you hoping to do after ordination, John?" His friend, Theodore, asked him one afternoon as the two of them were studying.

John leaned back in his chair and fiddled with his pencil thoughtfully. "Well, I'll serve wherever I'm sent. I hope it's somewhere close to home, but of course, I don't make that decision."

"You'll be an excellent parish priest," Theodore remarked. "You always give more than you take. That's exactly what a parish priest is supposed to do."

"Yes, and I want to help the poor especially, Ted. When I was younger, our family wasn't poor but we weren't well-off either. I know first-hand that even a simple word from a good priest can make a world of difference. But I'm still praying about what God wants me to do."

In his final year at the seminary, John was looking forward eagerly to his ordination. He had been assigned as an assistant pastor at a church not too far from his childhood home and was prepared for the joys and hardships of a priest's life. The evening before his ordination, his family and friends all came to be with him for dinner. They joked and laughed in celebration of the next day.
However, his father, Frank, began to feel guilty about enjoying himself so much. He pulled his son aside. "John, are you sure that we should be having a party on the eve of your ordination?"

"What else would be appropriate, Dad?"

Frank brought his eyebrows together in thought. "Well, shouldn't you be praying more? Preparing yourself mentally for tomorrow? I'm not sure if there are any rules on how an ordination is supposed to be..."

John threw his head back and laughed merrily. "There's no 'rule' to what happens on the eve of ordination. I can put your mind to rest, though, if you're worried that I'm not praying enough. I've prayed throughout my whole time here, and I'm excited and happy to be able to serve the Lord as one of His priests. There's nothing wrong with celebration- after all, Dad, this is an ordination, not a funeral."

After he became a priest, John went to serve at St. Genevieve's Church, in Elizabeth, NJ. He loved the people he served and knew that his choice to serve as a parish priest had been the right one. John began a Boy Scout troop for the young boys of his parish and took them on several outings. He wanted to give these young boys the benefit of good formation and healthy activities, the results of which he himself had discovered the fruits. They in turn loved Father Washington for it and the jubilant priest was a favorite among the boys.

Father Washington was transferred to St. Stephen's Church in Kearney, NJ. He was firm with his parishioners, just as he had been at St. Genevieve's, but his parishioners were grateful to be encouraged to know and love their Faith. John taught school for some of the children, and they all enjoyed his teaching style.

But this time of peace and joy was eventually obscured by a time of sadness and war as the United States was drawn into the conflict that had taken root in Europe and Asia. After the attack on Pearl Harbor, John asked permission from his pastor, a World War I veteran himself, to enlist as a chaplain and received his blessing.

Following this permission, John applied first for the Navy. The Navy turned him down, but the Army accepted him as a chaplain. After training, he applied to be sent overseas, and in November of 1942 went to Camp Myles Standish to await further orders.

Newspaper clipping from Long Beach, CA. This was placed in the local newspaper to announce the opening of the Four Chaplains' Sanctuary onboard the *Queen Mary*.

Included as part of the *Queen Mary* Sanctuary is a display case, holding various memorabilia. The red light shown in this picture is one of the emergency lights that were on the *Dorchester* lifejackets.

This stamp came out in honor of the Four Chaplains' sacrifice in 1948, five years after their death.

Portrait by Dick Levesque of *U-223*. *U-223* is the U-boat that torpedoed the *Dorchester*. More information about this painting can be found in the back of the book.

Mr. Dick Levesque was deeply inspired by the Four Chaplains' sacrifice at sea. He has painted three separate paintings about the disaster. His narrative can be found in the back of this book.

This is a copy of the Congressional document that in 1998 announced February 3 as Four Immortal Chaplains' Day. A copy of it is in the *Queen Mary*'s Sanctuary.

Portrait by Dick Levesque of the *Escanaba* picking up survivors. Used with permission.

Chaplain Rabbi Alexander Goode entered the war as a way to fight for the peace he had always wanted. Although it was hard to leave his family, Alex wanted to be a part of his dream.

Chaplain Father John Washington. The priest enlisted immediately after the Pearl Harbor attack and was known for the spectacles that he always wore. Father Washington became friends with many soldiers and encouraged them in their pursuits.

Chaplain Clark Poling grew up knowing the importance of prayer. His father was a well-known minister and encouraged his son in his goals. Dr. Poling told Clark that he believed entering as a chaplain was where God wanted him, and Clark agreed.

Chaplain George Fox's life taught him the value of perseverance. Even in the midst of overwhelming struggle, he continued to search for God's will. After Pearl Harbor, the WWI veteran entered the Second World War as a chaplain.

The USAT *Dorchester* was a former luxury liner converted to a troop ship in World War II. By 1943, she was well past her prime and every

voyage was risky. When she was struck by a German torpedo on February 3, 1943, only 230 out of 902 men survived.

There is a stained glass window of the Four Chaplains in the Pentagon Chapel. It was installed as a reminder of the chaplains' inspiration and legacy. A replica of the window is at the *Queen Mary*.

Chapter 6

~First Days~

"We were taken aboard, and got a look at that thing and it wasn't
your ideal dream cruise ship. It was a rust-covered thing, very
cramped, and it had been renovated to accommodate its passenger
capacity…Anyway, it was a dismal experience just to see this
place."[viii]

~James McAtamney, Dorchester survivor

January 23, 1943.

The USAT *Dorchester* sat in a New York harbor, patiently awaiting crowds of men to swarm her decks and prepare to leave. The men had no idea where they were going; that was to be kept secret until an undisclosed date. The *Dorchester*, the troops were assured, might look like a run-down old ship, but in reality, she would serve them well. The *Dorchester* had been in military service since February 1942, and before that, she had served as a passenger liner. This was simply a normal voyage for her.

The soldiers preparing to board were unaware of what was going on inside the New York Port of Embarkation, near Brooklyn. Colonel Fred Gillespie was hurriedly looking over a list of chaplains, trying to find two to leave on this voyage in two hours. At the very last minute, two chaplains had been taken off the list of those leaving.

"A frustrating situation," he grumbled to himself. "Looks like we still have our Protestant and Jew, but there's no one for the Catholics, and there are enough Protestants that they could use another one. Whom to pick?"

The list in front of Colonel Gillespie gave a bit of biographical information on each of the potential replacement chaplains. Gillespie looked a little closer, searching for a priest.

"Washington's from Newark," he noted as he saw the name of his own hometown. "I don't know him, but I'll put him on. And here…Poling! He's the son of Daniel Poling. The boys will be fortunate to have him."

It was a last-minute decision that happened to be perfectly aligned with Providence. The names were quickly sent off and preparations were in order for the *Dorchester*'s launch.

The *Dorchester* was almost unrecognizable from what she had looked like before the war. At that time, the *Dorchester* was a luxurious liner. But now, her halls were rusty and her paint was a dull grey.

A soldier nudged a buddy as he looked around. "Not all fancy now, huh Nick?"

The fellow in question turned, perturbed. "I never saw her when she was nice, Reggy. Did you?"

Reginald Walsh, known as Reggy to all his friends, laughed and shook his head. "Nope, but I heard she was a real beauty. Just look at her now, though! I'm not even sure this tug is safe, with them packing us all in here like sardines."

"Well, at least we're down here in E hold," Nick Fordsen reminded his friend. "Ben's in the upper holds. The bunks are stacked higher up there."

"And three high is better than four?" Reggy scoffed. He wasn't as eager to be optimistic as Nick. Bullied at school for being 'too small,' being a soldier was a way for Reginald Walsh to show the world that he was good enough for anything.

Nick shrugged good-naturedly; he was used to Reggy's mood swings. Throwing his duffel bag on a high bunk, he clapped the other lad on the shoulder. "Come on, stake your claim and then let's go up deck. I don't want to miss the launch."

At seven o'clock in the morning, crisp and clear, the *Dorchester* set sail. She was twenty-third in a convoy of sixty-four, heading east in anything but a straight line. The ships traveled in a zigzag pattern to avoid the German U-boats that prowled the North Atlantic. It was thought that traveling criss-cross made it more difficult for the Germans to track their position and then fire upon them.

It didn't take long for the four chaplains on board, Father John Washington, Clark Poling, Rabbi Alex Goode, and George Fox, to realize what a task they had been given. The four knew each other from Camp Myles Standish and got along magnificently. They were all humble-almost to a fault- and all exuded an air of parental guidance. The soldiers knew instinctively that these men would help whoever needed them, regardless of religious affiliation.

"Have you guys talked with any of the chaplains?" asked Ben Fordsen, Nick's older brother, as he leaned into the circle of three. Nick and Reggy both shook their heads. Ben looked at his hand of cards while he spoke, trying to decide which card to play. "They seem like good guys. My bunkmate, Will, is Jewish and he said that the rabbi, Goode is his name, I think, is planning to have Sabbath services during the voyage."

Reggy raised his eyebrows. "Where's he going to find the room for that? There's too many of us onboard to have any kind of organized event, and anyway, card games are taking up all the space."

A strong voice with the bit of an Irish brogue suddenly entered the conversation. "Would you men like your coffees refilled? There's a bit left in the pot."

The young men looked up in surprise at the priest. Nick was the first to smile at the older man. "Hello there, Father…Washington?"

"That's me," John Washington grinned back. "I'm Father John Washington. May I sit down with you boys?" he indicated to one of the chairs nearby.

Reggy stood up, a bit stone-faced but willing to chat with the man. He pulled a chair over. "Here you are, Padre. Take a seat."

"Thank you," said Father Washington. He didn't seem to notice the nickname that Reggy had given him, though the other boys did. "What are your names?"

Each of the men introduced himself individually, and Nick held up the cards. "Are you a card-player, Father? We can deal you in."

Father Washington shook his head with a smile. "Sorry lads, but I'll pass on this one. I'm not a big card-player."

The priest had grown up being taught that gambling was a waste of both time and money, and he had adopted the belief himself. He actually despised card-playing, but since he was trying to make friends with the men, Father Washington kept his views to himself.

"Not to change the subject, but I'm wondering if any of you are Catholic? I'll be offering Mass tomorrow morning at 0600," Father Washington said cheerfully. Nick and Ben nodded.
"I'll see you at Mass tomorrow morning, then. And Reggy, you're welcome to come, even though you aren't Catholic. Of course, the other chaplains will be holding other prayer services and the rabbi has his Sabbath service tonight."

Reggy looked at the priest, interested. "That's a nice offer for you to make, Father. I'm not really that religious, but I may tag along with Ben and Nick."

As Father Washington rose to leave, the Fordsen brothers looked at each other, surprised. It wasn't usual for Reggy to make any sort of remark about religion or Faith, unless the remark was a negative one. But they were even more astonished when Reggy shook his head and said, "He's an interesting man. I've never heard a priest be that respectful of other beliefs."

The card game was forgotten, and for a while the men sat and talked. They talked about their lives, their futures as soldiers, and about Father John Washington.

Chapter 7

~Storm Brewing~

"[The chaplains] were joking around, having a good time among themselves. We sat down and I told them about St. John's. And they said they have to get a master of ceremonies and they have to get ready because on the first of February they're gonna hold [talent] night. Nine acts, and very good acts."ix
~Michael Warish, Dorchester survivor

All the men agreed that the food on the *Dorchester* was tip-top. The problem was, hardly anyone on the ship could keep it down. Very few of the soldiers had ever been on a ship before, and they were all trying to get their "sea legs." The task proved more daunting than they had expected. Soldiers were hanging across the rails of the ship, trying to ignore the biting cold and as they vomited their breakfasts, lunches, and dinners into the seas.

The chaplains, though feeling just as sick as the other men, hurried around the ship to try to make them more comfortable. They carried bowls of soup for those who could hold down food; for others, they continued to sit by them and talk over their troubles.

After about six days, the men were excited to see land again. The day before, the convoy they had started out to sea with had left them to head to Russia. They were now sailing slowly toward Newfoundland. They didn't know why they were moving toward land- they were simply excited that it was in front of them.
"All troops, prepare to disembark with your packs. Repeating, all troops prepare to disembark." The message came across the loudspeakers clearly. There was a frenzy of activity as everyone prepared to leave.

"It's about time we got off that old boat," Reggy muttered discontentedly as he stomped through the snow beside Nick. "I was getting sick of it."

His more optimistic companion tried to cheer him up, saying, "Come on Reg, try to look at things through a brighter lens. We're going off to war, after all. It's not exactly meant to be a luxury trip."

The comment didn't make Reggy feel or act any better. He continued to mumble as they trudged off the ship and through the crisp snow. Suddenly, he looked up as a voice interrupted the sound of their breathing.

"Mind if I walk alongside you men?" The words came in a bit of a New York accent that Nick recognized as Rabbi Alex Goode. He smiled at the rabbi cheerfully and shook hands.

"How are you this morning, Rabbi? I'm Nick Fordsen, in case you don't remember me. There are a lot of names to memorize, I'm sure."

Alex threw his head back and laughed. It was jarring how happy he looked, snowflakes dusting his entire body. "There are certainly a lot of you, so thanks for the reminder, Nick. I'm well, though a bit cold. I'm sure you're pleased that we'll have some warm, solid, living quarters for a while."

The two chatted on while the other soldier frowned dismally. When they entered the bunk house, Reggy immediately fell onto one of the bunks and went straight to sleep.

The next morning, he woke up in a better mood. Reggy, Ben, and Nick, along with several other soldiers, trooped down to the mess hall together and got their breakfast of pancakes and coffee. After commenting again on the excellent cooking, they sat up to pay attention to the chaplains' announcements of the morning. Clark Poling was standing at the head of the room.

"Good morning men! Hope you're well and getting ready for a busy day. I want to let you all know about a decision that the other chaplains and I reached recently," he said cheerfully. "We're going to have a bit of a talent show on February 1st. So far, we have nine excellent acts and all of you are invited to be a part of the show. You can begin planning your acts and then talk to any of us chaplains to sign up."

The announcement put the room into a flurry of conversation, words whizzing about as soldiers tried to decide what they would do. But the announcement was soon put to the side in light of a more important fact that the men were now told that they were going to Greenland.

Michael Warish, a First Sergeant on the ship, put it bluntly, "Greenland is not green. Mother Nature offers no welcome mat. You don't have the area to play ball. You can't bat a ball there. If you want to pitch horseshoes, you're gonna have a problem putting the pegs in. If you want to go anywhere, there are no streets, no roads, and no paths. There's no power either. I've never seen so many candles in all my life. And the fleas and the gnats- they were so thick they get in your nostrils, in your mouth, in everything. You can hardly work. And after work? All you can do in Greenland is play poker."[x]

Poker wasn't too difficult an alternative for men who already gambled their hours away. But the cold temperatures and freezing weather didn't sound inviting. And for the chaplains, sitting in the ice surrounded by poker playing soldiers was not what they had envisioned when they enlisted. It wasn't that they wanted to be heroes in battle; they simply wanted to really aid in the war, and none of them felt that serving in Greenland would be doing that.

Clark wrote his feelings to his wife, Betty, "There is a part of my mind that is quite satisfied with the turn of events that sen[t] me to the safe but lonely post we have talked about. However, you know there is another part of me that is disappointed. Perhaps all of us are drawn to the heroic and hazardous. I have done all and more than is legitimate to get into the thick of it…Dearest, I love you, and wherever I go and for all time I am yours and you are mine. Read to Corky [Clark's nickname for his son, Clark Jr.] and spank him, love him, keep him away from the river, and feed him the oil! God bless you, my darling wife…"[xi]

January 29, the *Dorchester* was back to sea. This time, the journey went a little more smoothly. There were less seasickness and with two Coast Guard cutters a few miles away as escort, the men's fears were significantly qualmed.

Life upon the ship progressed in a monotonous pattern. Card playing and coffee drinking were the two main activities. The chaplains drifted about the ship, trying to engage the men in friendly conversation. They knew more about what was going on behind the ship's closed doors than the average soldier, making them slightly more on edge than all the others.

Unbeknownst to most everyone else on board, it was suspected the Allies' secret communication code had been cracked by the Germans. No one was sure, and it was assumed that the code was far too complex for it to have been solved, but the danger was still there.

Also, the *Dorchester* was preparing to enter an especially treacherous part of the North Atlantic known as Torpedo Junction. German U-boats were known to lie on the bottom of the ocean and many American ships had been taken down while en route to Europe.

But these fears were soon put to the side when a huge storm began to brew, only a couple of hours after they left the Newfoundland harbor. It started slowly, and then grew into a roaring gale, the likes of which few seasoned sailors had ever seen. Men tossed and turned in their bunks. No one was able to enter the galley because of all the broken dishes strewn about. Everything was chaos.

"It seems like the rest of our lives are going to be spent in the cold, wind, and rain," Nick murmured despondently.

Nothing but a groan came from the men around him. No one was strong enough to utter a word. Nick rolled over again, trying to find an almost comfortable position, when suddenly the door opened and Chaplain George Fox stumbled in.

Reggy, who was in one of the worst moods that he had been in while on the ship, turned angrily. "It may be Sunday, Fox, but none of us will be coming to services. Don't even bother asking! We're all sick as dogs." Nick flinched at his friend's angry words; it was obvious that the chaplain was just as green as the rest of them.

"I wasn't coming to urge you to attend services," the chaplain said while he tried to smile at the grumpy soldier. "I wanted to see if any of you need anything. The galley isn't open, but there's leftover soup and bread that could be brought if you wanted any."

Reggy turned over in his bunk. He didn't care what the chaplain or anyone else wanted, he simply wanted to sleep. His bunkmate, Peter, called out to the chaplain, "Any coffee?"

"There might be a little."

"If I can hold a mug without spilling it, coffee sounds good. Thanks for all your help, Chaplain Fox," Peter responded gratefully. After the chaplain left, Peter sat back on his mattress and frowned at the ceiling.

"What's wrong with you, Reg? Can't you see the man is trying to help?"

"Don't make me talk to you, Pete. I don't really feel like getting into a fight."

The other soldier simply sighed and waited for the cup of warm coffee. When Chaplain Fox stumbled back into the room, Peter got down from his bunk to take the cup from him.

"Thank you so much for getting this for me, Chaplain Fox. Do you care for any?"

The older man smiled but shook his head. "No, I'm fine. I don't think I could stand it anyway!"

Would you like to sit down?" Peter asked, motioning toward the bunks. "Not a very hospitable location I'm afraid, but it's the best we can do."

"I'd be pleased to rest a bit. Shall we have a visit?"

Surprised at the spontaneous yet heartfelt request, Peter nodded and settled back on the lower bunk. George Fox took a seat and prepared to listen to whatever the lonely soldier had to say.

Chapter 8

~Warnings~

"After this real severe storm, nothing was right. Men couldn't get back to the normal way of walking or doing anything because many of the men were very sick. And take into account, too, that many of these men, about seventy percent of them, [had] never before sailed in the North Atlantic."[xii]

~Michael Warish, Dorchester survivor

The storm that had tormented the men for two days slowly subsided and then went away completely on February 2. But as the soldiers started to feel better, the officials of the ship were thrown into a new sort of despondency.

At 15:30 PM on February 2, the *Dorchester* received a message from the commander of the Coast Guard Cutter *Tampa*, their escort. It read, "We are being followed. Submarines estimated in our vicinity. Inform all ships to close up tightly and stay closed for the night."[xiii] The message meant that the protective Coast Guard convoy with which the *Dorchester* traveled would circle close around them for the night.

An announcement was made at the mess hall that evening. "Announcement for all men on board. Repeat, announcement for all on board. A German submarine has been sighted and is following us. For safety precautions, everyone is ordered to sleep in full uniforms and lifejackets. Repeat, sleep wearing full uniforms and lifejackets. No exceptions. This is for your safety. Best of luck and you'll want to say your prayers tonight." Static followed the message. There was silence in the normally rowdy room.

Some of the soldiers stood up to leave, having lost their appetite. But Chaplain Poling stood up quickly. "Hold up men, the other chaplains and I wanted to make a quick announcement. I realize that some of you may not have noticed because of how nauseous you were feeling, but we had to skip our talent show because of the big storm. Now, it looks like everyone is feeling much better and we all have come to the agreement that we should have the show now. Who's ready?"

The chaplain's announcement was a surprise, but a pleasant one. It put the men in a cheerful mood, and for a couple of hours, the dangerous submarine was not the topic of conversation. But it never left anyone's mind; it was always there, making them all a little on edge.

The German submarine was again in the forefront of their minds when Chaplain Washington stood up from the piano, laughing merrily. "Good show men, that was enjoyable." His tone changed to a more somber one. "Now, please remember the captain's order as you prepare to bunk. We're going through hazardous territory, and when you hear an order like that, it means business. Sleep wearing everything you've got: uniform, boots, parka, and especially your lifejacket. Good night, and God bless."

Soldiers began to file out of the mess hall, eager to get back to their bunks and play cards. As they left, Father Washington called behind them, "I'll be in the chapel this evening to celebrate Mass. Any and all are welcome."

Back in their room, Nick sat on his bed. "I'm going to wait till the last minute to put all those clothes on. It must be 90 degrees or more down here."

Reggy, as usual, jeered at his friend's obedience. "Are you really going to wear all that to bed?"

"Of course," Nick snapped back, tired of his friend's determination to be glum. "That's the order I was given by my captain and I entered the army with a willingness to obey. Now if you don't mind, I'm going to the chapel."

"Suit yourself," came the retort.

Nick simply rolled his eyes and left the cabin. Ben joined him in the chapel, and both found that Mass took their minds off the dangerous submarine. After Mass was over and the boys said thanks to Father Washington, they headed back to their separate bunks.

Inside, nervous chatter permeated the atmosphere. Cards were being played to keep everyone's mind off the tension. Nick entered the room and immediately noticed the lieutenant cap that stood out among all of the other regular army men. He recognized the hat-wearer as Chaplain George Fox, and he seemed to be discussing something with Reggy. The two seemed to be in deep conversation and when Nick made eye contact with the chaplain, Fox shook his head. The sign was enough for him to leave and join a game of poker instead.

Almost a half hour later, Chaplain Fox stepped over to Nick. "You can go ahead now, sorry for the wait."

"No problem, thanks Chaplain," he said, hurrying over to his bunk. As Nick walked in, Reggy tipped his head up at Nick as if to say, "Hello." Then came the unexpected comment, "Hey, sorry Nick."

The words were highly unusual coming from Reggy. Nick stared at him in surprise and then sat down on the bed. "Mind if I ask what you and the chaplain were chatting about?"

"It was an interesting conversation. I'd seen Chaplain Fox earlier, but we'd never really had a conversation. He just walked in while I was sitting around and asked if we could talk. I said sure, even though I didn't particularly feel like chatting. He said that he had noticed that I seemed to be angry at someone or something and was wondering how he could help."

"Observant of him," Nick interjected.

"Not really," Reggy half smiled as he shifted positions. He still had his regular day clothes on- he hadn't put even a lifejacket on yet. "Anyway, he said that the chaplains have been drifting around the bunkrooms, visiting all of us soldiers, and he wanted to check in with me. We got into a bit of a conversation about him and his personal life."

"Really?" Peter, Reg's bunkmate, was now sitting by Nick. Both Nick and Peter were fully clothed and wearing their lifejackets, making a stark contrast to Reggy, who didn't seem to notice. "I'd love to hear. I spoke with Chaplain Fox yesterday and found him fascinating."

Reggy simply nodded and began to relate George Fox's life. During their conversation, Reggy had realized how much in common he had with the older chaplain. Much of the anger that Reggy had bottled up inside had been discussed with Chaplain Fox. Not a normal thing for the rigid 21 year old to talk about, but the chaplain had been so willing to listen that his story simply poured out.

Reggy told him about his difficult life at school, how he had been bullied by his classmates, and how entering the army was a way to show his worth. Chaplain Fox in turn spoke to him about his own experiences in the First World War and also his abusive home life. The two weren't searching for a solution to a problem, but instead were simply talking, man to man, about their lives. The conversation was a difficult one for Fox, because it brought back so many childhood memories, but he was glad to listen and share himself with a younger soldier.

"It sounds like he had a difficult time of it," Peter put in when Reggy had finished. Both Nick and Peter had listened the whole time; other soldiers, willing to do anything to take their minds off the lurking danger, had crowded around Reggy as well. Because the chaplains were so well loved by the community of men, everyone was interested in their lives before the war.

"I was talking with Clark Poling a couple days ago," said a soldier enthusiastically. "He said that when he was younger-"

The story was interrupted by a deafening crash and a moment later, everything went dark. Soldiers sitting on bunks were thrown backwards; those sleeping on the bottom bunks were crushed by the collapsing upper beds. No one knew what had happened. But few had remembered to obey their orders. Few were wearing lifejackets.

Chapter 9

~Twenty Minutes to Freezing~

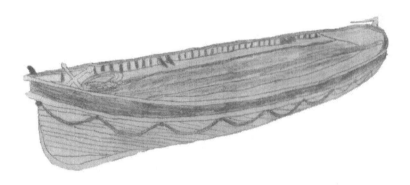

"*I raised my hand, and instead of saying 'Gotchya,' was going to snap the cards on the bunk, when everything went black and we couldn't even see each other. I said, 'We're hit!'*"[xiv]

~Walter Miller, Dorchester survivor

February 3, 1943. 12:55 AM.

The German U-boat U-223 dove 500 feet below waterline after firing three missiles. None of the German crew members knew who they had hit, or even if they had hit anyone. The captain knew how dangerous their situation was- if they had hit a ship, the convoy would surely be upon them in minutes.

On the *Dorchester*, all lights went out immediately, and water thundered in, assuring the *Dorchester*'s descent to the ocean. Those who survived the torpedo blast rushed above deck as they tried to escape from the chaotic and frightening scene below.

Nick Fordsen could barely move through the press of frantic soldiers, who were clamoring for the stairs. Inch by inch, he pushed through the crowd, crawled up the stairs, and finally arrived on deck. A blast of freezing air shocked him and made it impossible for him to think rationally for a moment. Coming back to his senses, Nick looked around him, trying to see through the thick darkness, trying to find his brother, or his bunkmate, or his best friend. The glow of a couple of flashlights was the only thing that made it possible to even make out facial features.

"Ben! Peter! Reggy!" The call was unheard through all the other shouts, screams, and yells of confusion that were all around him. As Nick looked around to find the boys however, he saw something else that disturbed him even more than the crash originally had. Most of the soldiers were hugging themselves, endeavoring to retain any body heat they had left. Some had only a shirt and pants on, a precious few had coats. Regardless of what they were wearing, very few had a lifejacket.

Nick punched a man next to him in the shoulder to get his attention. "Hey! Where's your lifejacket?"

The question was an unwelcome one. "Don't ask *me* where my lifejacket is! I didn't have a chance to grab it when the torpedo blasted…"

Shaking his head, Nick moved away from the man. Had anyone else followed the orders? Surely his brother Ben had- but he had no way of knowing if his assumption was true. The last time he had seen him was at Mass, and Ben didn't have a lifejacket on at that point. He had promised Nick that he would obey orders, but the younger man didn't know if he had followed through on the commitment. Nick continued to search, but he knew his efforts were in vain. The odds of finding his companions were slim to none, and the ship was rapidly taking on water.

***

When the crash had come, Reggy had narrowly missed being crushed by the bunks above him. He made it out just in time by catapulting himself to the opposite side of the room. The self-imposed lunge had left bruises, but it was better than being crushed under wood and metal.

Now, Reggy pushed himself among the desperate men. The man nearest him was crying pitifully, begging for his family. Another man leaned mutely against the deck wall, staring blankly out to sea. It was as though he was already dead.

"There's no time to waste," Reggy reminded himself sharply. "Keep moving, don't stop." He obeyed his own orders, but realized as he did so that he had not obeyed another set of orders earlier that evening. He was not wearing a lifejacket.

He was finally at topside and there was again no opportunity to wait. "Get out of the way," Reggy snarled to a young soldier.

Abruptly, a hand grabbed the back of his shirt. "Reggy!" The voice was distinct, sharp, and yet caring. Ready to have a fight on his hands, he turned around. "What-oh, Chaplain Fox. What are you doing out here?"

"Same thing you are. Where's your lifejacket?"

Reggy shrugged his shoulders and pretended not to care. "I forgot to put one on before coming up. I'll be fine."

Chaplain Fox saw past the bravado and looked kindly at the young soldier. "Reggy, get the men's attention and form a line. The other chaplains and I will be at the head, by the locker. It's full of lifejackets. Go first to Chaplain Goode- he'll hand you a lifejacket. Then continue to urge everyone else."

***

"Nick! Where are you?" Ben Fordsen shouted into the inky blackness that surrounded him. He was searching desperately for his younger brother, but to no avail. The bulky lifejacket he wore made it difficult for him to force his way through the crowd, but Ben pressed on in his search.

"Come over here, Ben, we need you," he heard his bunkmate, Will, call to him.

"Lead with your voice, Will. I can't tell where you are," Ben shouted back and continued to make his way through the swarms of men, this time in a different direction. He finally reached Will and grasped his arm. "What do you need?"

Will handed him an axe. "We need to break away this ice so we can get the lifeboat filled and into the water. It's more of a job than it looks." With his hand, he motioned for Ben to look down the deck. Adorning the sides of the rapidly sinking ship were thirteen lifeboats, the pulleys that held them were all encased with ice. The ice had to be broken away before the pulleys could function.

Ben swung the axe and threw everything he had into the blow. A jar went through his arms at the impact. "Unbelievable. This ice is as hard as steel...this is pointless."

"Do it anyway," Will yelled above the noise. "This is the only way that some men will survive. I heard one of the sailors say we probably only have about 20 minutes left till she sinks."

Though angry at the prospects in front of him, Ben recognized the truth in the answer. He continued to hit the ice, having pushed his search for Nick to the back of his mind.

Not enough time, Ben thought. There would never be enough time for lifeboats to be lowered and lifejackets to be issued. Behind him, he saw a line starting to form, for what he didn't know. But he turned back to his task and hit the frozen globe one more time, along with the two men by him.

A loud creak followed their efforts and the men shouted in anticipation at their success. But the excited shout quickly turned into a yell of horror as the pulleys flew out of their grasp and the boat toppled off the edge of the ship, into the icy water below. It had all been a waste of precious time and energy. Curses were hurled, blames were cast, but all the men realized that nothing could be done about the situation. They simply moved to the next lifeboat.

Chapter 10

~A Gift Too Precious~

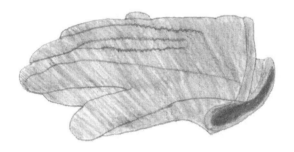

"One chaplain was shaking this one boy very hard…this boy was hysterical. He was screaming, and this chaplain was trying to get him to quiet down to talk to him. He said, 'I want you to take this jacket, get on the lifeline, and drop off the ship. You can save yourself.' Another chaplain was there beside him lowering the men, putting them on that lifeline."[xv]

~Roy Walters, Dorchester survivor

"Chaplain Poling! How many lifejackets are left?" Reggy called.

Clark Poling looked up and flashed the young solider a quick smile. "Not that many, Reggy. The rabbi is looking for more right now."

Reggy bit his lip in thought. "I could run down below to find some," he offered.

"Far too dangerous, and it would be impossible anyway," the chaplain told him. He handed a lifejacket to another soldier while he spoke.

Reggy went as quickly as he could over to where axes were flying. "It looks to me like that boat is just about ready to go. Am I right?"

"Reggy! Where's Nick?" Ben was elated to find a familiar face.

"I'm not sure, but I've been helping the chaplains," Reggy answered as he helped the men launch the lifeboat into the water. "They've formed a line to hand out lifejackets."

"Reggy, I need your help." Father Washington's voice came. "The ship will be submerged in about seven minutes and we must get lifejackets on these men. We need you to help hand them out."

"I'm coming, along with a friend of mine," Reggy called back and began to drag Ben with him.

The two got to the chaplains just in time. Ben grabbed ahold of several lifejackets and threw them into the remaining men's eager hands.

"Your hands look like they're in significant pain." Ben recognized the kind voice as Rabbi Goode's and he turned to respond.

"I'm fine; I've just been chopping ice. A bit cold, but so is everyone else." While he spoke, he looked down at his hands. They were red and chapped, with skin peeling off the knuckles.

Rabbi Goode pulled the gloves from his own hands and handed them to Ben. "These should help," he said matter of factly.

"No, you need them," argued Ben.

"I have another pair," said Rabbi Goode. He nodded at Ben to put them on, flashed him a quick smile, and then turned to speak with Chaplain Fox.

Ben gratefully slipped on the gloves. He reached down for a lifejacket, but his hands could find none.

"Chaplain Poling, do you have any lifejackets over there?" he hollered across the deck. No response came; Fox and Poling were too busy searching with Reggy for any lifejackets.

"Please, I have a wife and children at home. Aren't there any jackets left?" the man in front of Ben looked forlorn and dejected. The man knew that his chances of survival were slim at best.

Ben had just opened his mouth to utter the discouraging answer when without warning, Father Washington was next to him.

"Here's one," he said cheerfully. He untied the laces that secured the thick garment, pulled it over his head, and handed it to the man.

"No, Father! I didn't mean for you to give me yours."

The priest smiled. "Nonsense, Fields. It's my job. Now don't waste any more time. When you're in the water, pull on the string you see on your right. A red light will appear and will help the Coast Guard cutters rescue you when they arrive. Godspeed!" He pushed the distraught man, who slipped the jacket on. His face showed a mixture of disbelief and gratitude.

Ben, who had witnessed the whole incident, was too shocked to speak. Time seemed to move slowly. He saw, as if in a daze, the other three chaplains remove their lifejackets in a similar fashion. They spoke softly and compassionately to the men whom they aided, yet were completely firm in their resolve.

A rough clap on the back jolted Ben back into the frantic pace of the moment. He felt two people flanking him. "Nick, when did you get here?" Ben asked his brother, hugging him tightly.

"I've been up here the whole time," Nick stammered. He had been in the biting temperature for so long that he was beginning to feel the effects of the weather. "Reggy found me and led me here."

"Did you see what they just did?" Ben was almost hysterical now. He ran over to George Fox and shook him by the shoulder. "Chaplain, you have to take my life vest, please! There's no way you'll be able to survive out there."

Fox smiled, if a bit sadly, at the young boy in front of him. Ben reminded him of his own son, Wyatt. "It's all right, lad. I can't take your lifejacket and I can assure you that none of these other men will either."

Nick now joined his brother and didn't let the chaplain finish. "Chaplain Fox, you all have given every lifejacket away, even your own!"

Reggy felt a lump in the back of his throat as he realized what he had just witnessed. He and many others were wearing jackets now- jackets they wouldn't have needed if they had only obeyed orders. And here stood the four chaplains. Four men who had obeyed orders. Yet they stood here without jackets themselves, having given their own to others.

The words were enough and didn't have to be repeated. "Thank you," was all Reggy could utter with his hoarse voice. The rabbi stepped over and pulled on Reggy's lifejacket string, the movement causing a bright red flash of light.

"Take care of yourself and may God be with you."

Each of the chaplains had said the same words to every person they had helped. *God be with you. Godspeed.* Reggy thought about the words as he ran down the deck, pushing until he got to the bow. He looked around, trying to see Ben and Nick. When he wasn't able to see them, Reggy looked at the churning sea below him. But this wasn't the time for cowardly thoughts. The chaplains had given him a chance to live and it was his responsibility to take the shot. But the instant he was about to take the leap, a sound from behind made him stop.

They were singing. Alex Goode and George Fox. John Washington and Clark Poling. They had their arms linked and they were singing. Reggy took a couple of steps toward them, straining to hear the words.

Eternal Father, strong to save,
Whose arm hath bound the restless wave,
Who biddest the mighty ocean deep
Its own appointed limits keep;
Oh, hear us when we cry to Thee,
For those in peril on the sea!

The simple words created a kaleidoscope of memories. Sitting in church, next to his grandmother. Opening the red hymnal and finding the Sunday hymn. His mother whispering to him, "It's a song for sailors, Reggy. It's a prayer for their protection and safety while away." How appropriate a song to be singing now. When all seemed to be lost, four ordinary men had done an extraordinary thing, Reggy thought. They had given more than they took from others. They had given a reason to hope.

All the thoughts took only a second to remember, and then they were whisked away with the cutting wind. The song completed, Reggy turned back toward the edge of the ship. It wouldn't be a jump now; it would be more of a step off the edge. But before he moved, Reggy heard, above the deafening crash of the waves, four strong voices mixing together. Father Washington was praying in Latin. Clark Poling and George Fox were praying the Our Father in unison. Rabbi Alex Goode was praying a Hebrew prayer.

Their voices mixed with the sleet and caused Reggy to pause once again. Whispering the words of the Our Father under his breath, he took a running leap and cannon-balled into the North Atlantic.

Epilogue

~Four Immortal Chaplains~

"I was on a life raft and when [the ship] rolled over, that's when I saw the four chaplains, [who] had climbed up on the keel and they were standing arm in arm. And then she nosed [and] they slid off into the water." [xvi]

~James Eardley, Dorchester survivor

It looked like a Christmas tree, a deadly, grim Christmas tree.

Red lights, glistening in the darkness. Desperate men, shivering in the icy water. Hypothermia, taking lives not ready to go. Would no one come to rescue them?

The *Escanaba*, one of the Coast Guard cutters, had been rushing toward the scene until the lieutenant commander made them stop. "We must wait for orders to pick up survivors," he said in a voice clearly tormented by the need for obedience. "We have been specifically instructed not to stop for anything until Greenland because of the immense danger. We have to be given orders to pick up the men."

The men onboard the ship that was supposed to save the *Dorchester* and her survivors were tormented over the decision. But orders were orders, they knew. When finally the signal was cleared, the *Escanaba* rushed to where the red lights dotted the ocean.

The *Dorchester*'s soldiers had been in the water over a half-hour longer than was thought possible for hypothermia victims to survive. Because those who were alive were too weak to do anything, even to grasp a rope, crew members of the cutter donned wet suits and jumped into the water below. The rescuers took men floating on the water before others in boats and rafts, as these were at a higher risk of freezing to death.

Few of the men floating in the water were still alive or able to be saved. Most of the survivors were from the lifeboats and others on rafts. The survivors were badly frozen and hypothermic. None of the four chaplains were ever found.

***

Back in the United States, the chaplains' wives received the news of their husband's deaths. Each had her own reaction to the loss. Isadore Fox was stunned and almost unable to function for several days after receiving the news. She said "[After the telegram] I did not want to live without George. Although I love my children dearly, with George gone there seems to be a gap of a million miles between the children and me." [xvii]

One of the most difficult aspects of the loss for Isadore was the media attention. Everyone wanted to speak to the wives of the four heroic chaplains, whose story had been relayed by many survivors. One reporter told Isadore that her husband was a hero. Broken and grieving her enormous loss, she responded, "I always knew he was a hero, the way he worked in those small churches and never complained, even when the pay was so small that he could not get proper food for his children. I don't want a hero, I want my husband."[xviii]

Betty Poling, Clark's happy wife, thought that the Western Union man was bringing her Valentine's Day greetings from her husband. He wasn't. It was a heart-wrenching message instead: "The Secretary of War deeply regrets to inform you…" Eventually, Betty did receive her Valentine's gift- a little girl, Susan, named after Clark's mother. Clark would never meet this little girl named after the woman he loved so much.

Mary Washington, the mother of Father John Washington, deeply grieved her son's death. She received a telephone call from the War Department and began to scream in anger, pain, and grief. But this wasn't to be the end of her sufferings; after the news of John's death, she received the news that her other two sons, Francis and Leo, had also been killed in the war. Mrs. Washington was inconsolable, and following the news, she never left her house again.

Theresa Goode was getting little Rosalie ready to buy her a new pair of stockings when suddenly the family telephone rang. Her sister informed her that Alex's ship had been torpedoed, and that Alex was not a survivor. Theresa couldn't believe the news and struggled with the realization that she would never again see her husband. But soon, she was able to start moving on with her daughter and eventually married again, this time to Rabbi Harry Kaplan.

But after the war, the families of the chaplains realized how much their story resonated with the American people. A U.S. postal stamp came out in their honor five years later, although it was against custom to issue a stamp honoring a person until ten years after they were deceased. A new medal, the Chaplain's Medal of Honor, was issued posthumously to the chaplains and this medal will never be issued again. It is an honor reserved for these four men alone.

Theresa Goode, along with her daughter Rosalie, helped to begin the Four Immortal Chaplain's Foundation. It is an organization still in existence today, committed to spreading the message of ecumenism and interfaith in action through the Four Chaplain's legacy.

In an interview with the author, Ben Epstein told the story of the *Dorchester* in his own words, only months before his death in January 2013. He put the chaplains' sacrifice this way, "Did I do it? Did anyone else do it? No. They all had families, just like we did...But still they gave their lifejackets. Incredible. Just incredible."[xix]

~Historical Notes~

"Nemo potest dare quid non habet."
"No one can give that which he does not have."
~old Latin saying.

The story of the Four Immortal Chaplains was popular and widely circulated directly after the war ended. But even though their story is still told to all military chaplains at chaplains' school, the majority of Americans are unaware of these men's sacrifice at sea.

I didn't know about them either, until my younger sister did a simple Internet search on "World War 2 chaplains." She saw something that looked interesting and my mom came to look at it with her. A few clicks later, we had found some new Titanic Heroes. I looked into their story more, contacted one of the chaplain's relatives (Mr. David Fox-Brenton), and quickly decided that it was time to start writing a new book.

There has been very little written on the four chaplain's story, which obviously makes it difficult to find substantial research on their lives. But with the help of David Fox-Brenton (George Fox's great-nephew), the Immortal Chaplain's Foundation, and the generosity of the RMS *Queen Mary*, I was privileged enough to be able to do some on-site research for this book about the Four Chaplains that targets middle-school age readers.

On our trip to Long Beach, CA, my family and I were able to tour the *Queen Mary* with the impressive Commodore Everette Hoard, whose love for his ship is heart-warming and absolutely genuine. The main reason for seeing the beautiful liner-turned-museum was to tour the Four Chaplain's Sanctuary, a memorial chapel dedicated to these four men who gave their lives on February 3, 1943. The small room was filled with memorabilia from the chaplain's lives and paintings that illustrated the *Dorchester*'s final minutes. The experience helped me form a clearer picture of what those twenty five minutes must have been like for the 902 men onboard the doomed ship, 206 of which would survive the disaster.

Why does the *Queen Mary* have a Four Immortal Chaplains Sanctuary? Later on in World War II, the German U-boat *U-223* was itself sunk by the Allies in 1944. Survivors of the accident were transported to the United States as Prisoners of War on the *Queen Mary* herself. When the story of the Four Immortal Chaplains became well-known, and when others became aware that the *Queen Mary* had a link to the Four Chaplains, it was decided that a sanctuary would be installed onboard the ship, by then a museum and tourist attraction. The sanctuary is beautiful and a fitting tribute to these four extraordinary men. The *Queen* has a fascinating World War II history of her own, and I highly recommend touring this wonderful piece of American history. You will be shocked by how much you learn and see on the *Queen Mary*.

Back home, the experience added to the excitement of starting a new book. This one proved more difficult to write, but the *Queen Mary* research helped tremendously, as did Dan Kurzman's book *No Greater Glory*.

So, in my book, what is fact and what is fiction? All information in the first four chapters of the book about the men as individuals is from information found through interviews with the chaplain's family members and books written by them as well. Any quotes are from the same source- memoirs, books, and letters.

Dan Kurzman's book, *No Greater Glory*, proved invaluable in the writing of my book. His book, written in 2004, was truly the first book to go over the four chaplains as individual people, then look at them as brothers onboard the *Dorchester*, and finally document their heroic sacrifice. In the course of Dan Kurzman researching for his book, Mr. David Fox-Brenton did numerous interviews with survivors, which helped provide information about the chaplains and the *Dorchester*. These interviews provide the sources for most of the quotes in my book and have been used with permission from Mr. Fox-Brenton. Dan Kurzman passed away on December 12, 2010, thus I was sadly not able to speak with him personally.

The story of Ben Fordsen, Reginald Walsh, and Nick Fordsen is based upon survivor accounts and what, from my research, I believe the *Dorchester*'s journey would have been like for the soldiers on board. These men are not based on any specific survivors; as individuals, they are from my imagination entirely. Interactions with the men and the four chaplains are again from my imagination, but are based on survivor accounts that say how the chaplains interacted with the men.

Descriptions of the USAT *Dorchester* are taken from a variety of sources, including the aforementioned book and several historical websites. There are very few to no accounts of what the ship looked like inside, so this was based primarily on historical fact and what other transport ships at the time looked like. Visiting the *Queen Mary* aided in this as well, since the *Queen* herself was also an important transport ship in World War II. She was called the Grey Ghost, and Hitler himself wished her sunk, placing the highest bounty on her.

In July of 2012, I had the immense pleasure and privilege of interviewing the charming Mr. Ben Epstein, the last survivor of the *Dorchester*. I spoke with Mr. Epstein over the phone and it was evident from the beginning of our half-hour long conversation that the experience onboard the *Dorchester* was still fresh in this man's mind.

Mr. Epstein documented what it was like for him and his best friend onboard the ship. He specifically remembered the four chaplains in the morning of February 3, and what it was like for them to take the leap into the ocean. It was surprising to me how much Mr. Epstein was still moved by his story, and by the Four Chaplains' sacrifice, even though it had been decades since the incident. The time we spent on the telephone was one of the highlights of researching for this book.

Sadly, Ben Epstein recently passed away, in January 2013. He was the last known survivor of the USAT *Dorchester*. Mr. Epstein dedicated his life to telling the story of the Four Chaplains, and he did so through public speaking, interviews, and various other modes of communication. When I learned of Mr. Epstein's death, it was even more apparent how much of a gift I had been given through my interview.

I was also able to interview Mr. Dick Swanson, one of the men who rescued the survivors of the *Dorchester*. His testimony was sobering and it was apparent that, like Ben Epstein, the images from that morning would be forever imprinted in his mind. Mr. Swanson, like most of the rescuers aboard the two Coast Guard Cutters, stated that because of all the red lifejacket lights dotting the water, the water looked like a Christmas tree. That image alone spoke volumes of how utterly human the scene was, and how superhuman the chaplains' sacrifice.

Mr. Swanson recalled that virtually all of the survivors were far too weak to even grasp a rope. Having stayed in the water about a half-hour longer than it is thought hypothermia victims can survive, the rescuers had a difficult task on their hands. Dick Swanson stated that for the first time, Coast Guard crewmen donned wetsuits and swam in the water to rescue the men. This mode of rescue later became what we now know as Coast Guard rescue swimmers. Being able to interview this man, who saved the lives of so many on February 3, 1943, was a true honor and I hope to be able to speak with him more.

The Four Chaplains' story is one that more people need to know. It's a story of heroism, self-sacrifice, and willingness to give more than we take. Their example is one that we should all strive to imitate, and they are truly Titanic Heroes. My hope is that through reading this book, you have discovered just how significant this tale is and how important that it continue to be told. If you would like more information about the chaplains, please read Dan Kurzman's book, *No Greater Glory*. You can also visit the Immortal Chaplains Foundation at: www.immortalchaplains.org. Also, visit www.TitanicHeroes.com to learn more about the Four Chaplains and their sacrifice.

~Acknowledgements~

"No one who achieves success does so without acknowledging the help of others. The wise and confident acknowledge this help with gratitude."

-Alfred North Whitehead.

To David Fox-Brenton. Ever since we first spoke over the phone about the Four Chaplains, you've been incredibly helpful and supportive of this project. The research you've done and the insight you have into this story has made it possible for me to access information about the Chaplains that I wouldn't otherwise have. Thank you!

To Richard Swanson and (the late) Ben Epstein. Thank you both for your willingness to speak with me about your experiences. You both were charming and wonderful over the phone, and the interviews helped me establish a real-life connection to this story.

To Dick Levesque. Thank you so much for being so generous with your paintings! Ever since I first saw your painting of the Dorchester's sinking, I knew it was something I wanted in my book. Your paintings are beautiful and I'm so thankful that you allowed me to include them.

To Julia Fogassy. Sometimes, even the best ideas don't work out. When you first told me that you wanted me to 'hit delete and start over,' I wasn't all that excited, but you have a track record of being right about these things. And as usual, you were one hundred percent correct. This book wouldn't look anything like it does now without your critique, help, and edits. Thank you so much!

To Commodore Everette Hoard and the RMS *Queen Mary* tour manager. When I first called the *Queen Mary*, I had no idea that the response would be so positive. From the start, you were happy to listen, pleased to help, and offered your services willingly. Your generosity in providing me and my whole family with tickets to the entire ship was overwhelming, and the experience provided unbelievable on-site research for this book.

Commodore Hoard, meeting you and being able to tour your ship was really special. Every time you mentioned the *Queen*, I could tell how much she meant to you. You gave me information about the ship that I wouldn't have been privy to with any other tour. It was such a pleasure to meet you and talk with you.

To my mom, Tena Crosby. Thank you so much for working with me on this project and being willing to let me take the time I needed. Your edits were extremely helpful and your encouragement to get it done made it get finished in time. I love you- thank you!

To my brother, Benjamin Crosby. Since art and graphic design isn't my forte whatsoever, I need someone that's happy to help me in that area. I absolutely love the covers you've made for me and the drawings that are in the each of the chapters look great. I love you…thanks a bunch.

To the Four Immortal Chaplains. Your story of heroism has inspired me and my whole family. Thank you for your sacrifice and your ability to give more than you took. Your legacy lives on!

~Picture Credits~

"What I like about photographs is that they capture a moment that's gone forever, impossible to reproduce."[xx]

~Karl Lagerfield

The Army pictures of the Four Chaplains were shot by a US government official for official duties and employed for government use, thereby allowing them to fall under the public domain. The picture of the USAT *Dorchester* was taken from the public domain as well, having been prepared by a US government official and used for US Army work. The image of the stamp that was released in honor of the Four Chaplains is also in the public domain because it was prepared by a US government official.

All pictures from the RMS *Queen Mary* were taken by me and my family, during our trip in September 2012. These pictures therefore belong to us and all copyright is reserved.

I contacted Mr. Dick Levesque in January 2013, in order to talk with him about his beautiful paintings of the *Dorchester*. Mr. Levesque has painted three portraits to commemorate the sinking and each picture is unique. I asked him if I could have permission to use the pictures in my book, and he graciously allowed me to do so. These pictures have not been used in any other book about the USAT *Dorchester* and I am honored to be able to have them in mine.

The following is a narrative written by Dick Levesque, describing his portraits about the *Dorchester*. I am deeply honored by his willingness to send me these pictures and his narrative gives insight into thought behind the portraits.

"My name is Dick Levesque and I am a retired Coast Guardsman and Marine Artist. I have previously read accounts of the *Dorchester* sinking and the remarkable ultimate sacrifice that that the four Army Chaplains gave on that bitterly cold morning of February 3, 1943. Most of my marine artwork revolves around historical events that pertain to the U.S. Coast Guard. While researching the history of the *USCGC Escanaba* I became intrigued again with the *Dorchester* incident. I knew that I wanted to portray both ships but was unsure how I was going to go about it. I tried some rough sketches at first showing the sinking but I felt that this was too gruesome.

I even attempted depicting hundreds of men floating among the wreckage struggling for survival with others lifelessly adrift being held up only by their life preservers. I rejected this also as it seemed too disrespectful to these poor souls and the families that might have the opportunity to view the finished painting. My research had indicated that the *Dorchester* sank rapidly shortly after midnight with one survivors account stating "it was a moonless night and bitterly cold". There was no fire visible when she slipped below the surface and another account indicates that "star flares" were fired about 45 minutes after the sinking. This would make a portrayal of the sinking very difficult as there was no illumination for some time.

I shelved the project for many months randomly wondering how I could complete this painting. One evening while dozing off to sleep it suddenly hit me that the most reverent way was to show both vessels in their glory the day before this tragedy.
After a very restless sleep I awoke and could hardly wait to begin. I had all the research information on both vessels and hastily put it to paper to see if it "worked".

It did and I think it honors all those involved including the *CGC Comanche* barely visible on the left horizon. I have received reviews such as *"You have really set the stage for one of WW11's major tragedies. The sea, sky, color, all puts You in mind that something bad is going to happen. Sadly, it did!"* and *"it brings a chill to see the Dorchester in the background, knowing what would happen soon afterward"* and finally "Y*ou can almost feel a bitter cold wind. You can look at the picture and wonder what those guys must have been feeling and what was about to happen"*. I am very pleased with the results and feel blessed to have been able to pay tribute to the four Chaplains and ALL that gave their lives that fateful day.

As a sad footnote to this painting, the *CGC Escanaba*, who rescued the majority of the *Dorchester* survivors, herself succumbed to the enemy on June 13, 1943 the victim of a floating mine. The explosion and sinking claimed all but two of her crew. Only one survives today."

~Endnotes~

"The wisdom of the wise, and the experience of ages, may be preserved by quotations."[xxi]

~Isaac D'Israeli

[i] Transcript from interviews conducted by David Fox-Brenton with survivors. 2003 to 2004. Used with permission.

[ii] Transcript from interviews conducted by David Fox-Brenton with survivors. 2003 to 2004. Used with permission.

[iii] Transcript from interviews conducted by David Fox-Brenton with survivors. 2003 to 2004. Used with permission.

[iv] Transcript from interviews conducted by David Fox-Brenton with survivors. 2003 to 2004. Used with permission.

[v] Transcript from interviews conducted by David Fox-Brenton with survivors. 2003 to 2004. Used with permission.

[vi] Transcript from interviews conducted by David Fox-Brenton with survivors. 2003 to 2004. Used with permission.

[vii] Transcript from interviews conducted by David Fox-Brenton with survivors. 2003 to 2004. Used with permission.

[viii] Transcript from interviews conducted by David Fox-Brenton with survivors. 2003 to 2004. Used with permission.

[ix] Transcript from interviews conducted by David Fox-Brenton with survivors. 2003 to 2004. Used with permission.

[x] Transcript from interviews conducted by David Fox-Brenton with survivors. 2003 to 2004. Used with permission.

[xi] Transcript from interviews conducted by David Fox-Brenton with survivors. 2003 to 2004. Used with permission.

[xii] Transcript from interviews conducted by David Fox-Brenton with survivors. 2003 to 2004. Used with permission.

[xiii] Transcript from interviews conducted by David Fox-Brenton with survivors. 2003 to 2004. Used with permission.

[xiv] Transcript from interviews conducted by David Fox-Brenton with survivors. 2003 to 2004. Used with permission.

[xv] Transcript from interviews conducted by David Fox-Brenton with survivors. 2003 to 2004. Used with permission.

[xvi] Transcript from interviews conducted by David Fox-Brenton with survivors. 2003 to 2004. Used with permission.

[xvii] Transcript from interviews conducted by David Fox-Brenton with survivors. 2003 to 2004. Used with permission.

[xviii] Transcript from interviews conducted by David Fox-Brenton with survivors. 2003 to 2004. Used with permission.

[ixx] Transcript from a personal interview with Ben Epstein. Late 2012.

[xx] Lagerfield, Karl. "What I like about Photographs Is That They Capture a Moment That's Gone Forever, Impossible to Reproduce." *Goodreads*. N.p., n.d. Web. 16 Feb. 2013.

xx Chesterton, Gilbert K. "I Had Always Felt Life First as a Story: And If There Is a Story There Is a Story-teller." *Goodreads*. N.p., n.d. Web. 16 Feb. 2013.

xxi D'Israeli, Isaac. "The Wisdom of the Wise and the Experience of Ages May Be Preserved By Quotations." *Goodreads*. N.p., n.d. Web. 26 Feb. 2013.

~About the Author~

"I had always felt life first as a story: and if there is a story there is a story-teller."[xxii]

~GK Chesterton

Cady Crosby is fifteen years old and homeschooled. Her passions are writing, public speaking, and reading good literature. She lives with her parents, Robert and Tena Crosby, and her five siblings in Washington state. This is Cady's second book. Her first, *A Titanic Hero: Thomas Byles*, is about Father Thomas Byles and his heroic actions while onboard the RMS *Titanic*. It is available through TitanicHeroes.com and Amazon.com.

Cady and her brother, Benjamin, have started a non-profit corporation called Titanic Heroes™. Titanic Heroes™ exists to teach and inspire others to learn and live the 3G Principles (GIVE what you have, GIVE more than you take, and GIVE it your all) by sharing stories of historical heroism. They tour around the country with multi-media presentations, showcasing the stories of real heroism and real sacrifice throughout history. Last year, they focused primarily on the RMS *Titanic* and the heroes onboard the ship that night. In 2013, they have added a new presentation is on the Four Immortal Chaplains and their heroic story

For more information on Cady's work, please visit: www.TitanicHeroes.com.

Made in the USA
Charleston, SC
13 May 2014